FEATURING THE ARTWORK OF

# THOMAS KINKADE

CELEBRATING THE BLESSINGS
*of* LOVED ONES

# GARDEN OF
# FRIENDSHIP

THOMAS KINKADE *Painter of Light*™

THOMAS NELSON PUBLISHERS®
Nashville

# The Garden of Friendship

Published in Nashville, Tennessee, by Thomas Nelson, Inc.

Scripture quotations are from the NEW KING JAMES VERSION of the Bible. Copyright © 1979, 1980, 1982, Thomas Nelson, Inc., Publishers.

Scripture quotations noted NIV are taken from the HOLY BIBLE, NEW INTERNATIONAL VERSION ®. Copyright ©1973, 1978, 1984 by International Bible Society. Used by permission of Zondervan Bible Publishing House. All rights reserved.

The "NIV" and "New International Version" trademarks are registered in the United States Patent and Trademark Office by International Bible Society. Use of either trademark requires the permission of International Bible Society.

Design and production by: Quebecor World Digital Services, Chicago

ISBN 0-7852-6845-6

**Printed in the United States of America**
8 9 10 - 05 04 03 02 01

# $\mathcal{P}$resented to:

_____

On this ___14^th___ day

of ___May___

By ___Marian Longshore___

With this special message:

___We have had many years___
___with our husbands, going___
___out to eat spending New___
___Years together - We were___
___always depending on each___
___other in bad times and___
___good.___

∽

3

A single rose can be my garden . . .
a single friend, my world.

— Leo Buscaglia

The glory of friendship is not in the outstretched hand,
nor the kindly smile, nor the joy of companionship;
it is in the spiritual inspiration that comes to one
when he discovers that someone else believes in
him and is willing to trust him.

— Ralph Waldo Emerson

He who covers a transgression seeks love,
but he who repeats a matter separates friends.

— Proverbs 17:9

# Our times together
## are such precious memories for me.

~

_____

_____

_____

_____

_____

_____

_____

_____

_____

_____

_____

Friendship is the inexpressible comfort of
feeling safe with a  person, having neither
to weigh thoughts nor measure words.

– GEORGE ELLIOT

The proper office of a friend is to side
with you when you are in the wrong.
Nearly everyone will side with you when
you are in the right.

– MARK TWAIN

Thomas
Kinkade

Sutter Creek Inn

Developing a servant's heart can be one of the most satisfying undertakings of your life. The more you learn to focus on blessing others, the more freely the blessings will flow in your life.

– THOMAS KINKADE

To know that I have helped someone a little or made a day brighter will make my own work easier and cause the sun to shine on the dark days, for we all have them. 'Tis then a little place of sunshine in the heart helps mightily. And there is nothing that puts so much brightness there as having helped someone else.

– AUTHOR UNKNOWN

From quiet homes and first beginning,

Out to the undiscovered ends,

There's nothing worth the wear of winning,

But laughter and the love of friends.

– HILAIRE BELLOC

A mirror reflects a man's face, but what he
is really like is shown by the kind of friend
he chooses.

– PROVERBS 27:19 TLB

Real friendship is shown in times of
trouble; prosperity is full of friends.

– EURIPIDES

A good cause is often injured more by
ill-timed efforts of its friends than by the
arguments of its enemies. Persuasion,
perseverance and patience are the best
advocates on questions depending on the
will of others.

– THOMAS JEFFERSON

Friends and good manners will carry you where
money won't go.

– MARGARET WALKER

Never lose sight of the fact that the most important
yardstick of your success will be how you treat other
people – your family, friends, and coworkers, and even
strangers you meet along the way.

– BARBARA BUSH

The antidote for fifty enemies is one friend.

– ARISTOTLE

A blessed thing it is for any man or woman to have a friend, one human soul whom he can trust utterly, who knows the best and worst of us, and who loves us in spite of all our faults.

– CHARLES KINGSLEY

A gossip separates close friends.

– PROVERBS 16: 28

The most I can do for my friend is simply be his friend.

– HENRY DAVID THOREAU

I intentionally seek out companions who enjoy good conversation and positive activities; people who, like me, believe that life still offers a lot to be hopeful about and that many of the problems in the world are fixable.

– THOMAS KINKADE

We cannot tell the precise moment when friendship is formed. As in filling a vessel drop by drop, there is at last a drop which makes it run over. So in a series of kindness there is, at last, one which makes the heart run over.

– JAMES BOSWELL

No two persons see people and things alike. What we see and how we see depend upon the nature of light.

– LAURA INGALLS WILDER

It is wise to apply the oil of refined politeness to the mechanism of friendship.

– COLETTE

# I *am so grateful that God has allowed us to spend time together as friends.*

❧

_____

_____

_____

_____

_____

_____

_____

_____

_____

_____

# I have counted on you like family. Thanks for being there for me during the difficult times.

~

You and John were with us in 1978 when Jack and I were both in the hospital.

Friendship is unnecessary, like philosophy, like art. . .
It has no survival value; rather it is one of those things
that give value to survival.

– C. S. LEWIS

I still find each day too short for the thoughts I want to
think, all the walks I want to take, all the books I want
to read and all the friends I want to see.

– JOHN BURROUGHS

A friend is one who walks in when the rest
of the world walks out.

– WALTER WINCHELL

My only sketch, profile, of Heaven is a
large blue sky, and larger than the biggest I
have seen in June--and in it are my
friends--every one of them.

– EMILY DICKINSON

Thomas Kinkade

It is true that we find ourselves reflected
in our friends and neighbors, and if we
are in the habit of having bad neighbors,
we are not likely to find better by changing
our location.

– LAURA INGALLS WILDER

A man cannot be said to succeed in this
life who does not satisfy one friend.

– HENRY DAVID THOREAU

# Please know how much
## I appreciate our friendship.

~

(She was 13)

Remember when Linda
was left in Ohio
    We called you at
12 midnight and John
+ you. went with us
to King's Island to pick
her up. We got home
@ 6$^{30}$Am after eating Breakfast

A faithful friend is an image of God.

– FRENCH PROVERB

Remember to be yourself and to surround
yourself with people and things that define
and reflect who you are.

– THOMAS KINKADE

# Thank you for all your encouragement.
## Your confidence means so much.

❧

_____

_____

_____

_____

_____

_____

_____

_____

_____

_____

_____

# Our times together
# are such precious memories for me.

❧

_____

_____

_____

_____

_____

_____

_____

_____

_____

_____

_____

# I *am so grateful that God has allowed us to spend time together as friends*

❧

_____

_____

_____

_____

_____

_____

_____

_____

_____

_____

_____

_____

Some by their bad temper and
exacting dispositions estrange their
relatives and repel friendly advances.
Than they shall bewail the fact that
their friends are so few.

– LAURA INGALLS WILDER

A decent boldness ever meets
with friends.

– HOMER

Thomas Kinkade

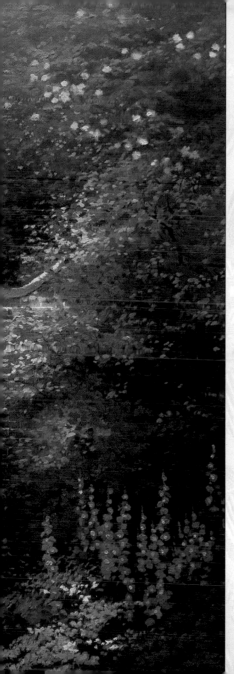

A friendship founded on business is better than a business founded on friendship.

– JOHN D. ROCKEFELLER JR.

A false friend and a shadow attend only while the sun shines.

– BENJAMIN FRANKLIN

Every man should have a fair sized cemetery in which to bury the faults of his friends.

– HENRY WARD BEECHER

Every man passes his life in the search
after friendship.

– RALPH WALDO EMERSON

Friendship without self-interest is one of
the rare and beautiful things of life.

– JAMES F. BYRNES

Tell me what company thou keepest,
and I'll tell thee what thou art.

– MIGUEL DE CERVANTES

I didn't find my friends; the good Lord
gave them to me.

– RALPH WALDO EMERSON

# Please know how much
## I appreciate our friendship.

‿

_____

_____

_____

_____

_____

_____

_____

_____

_____

_____

_____

We have been friends together in sunshine
and in shade.

– Caroline Sheridan Norton

The language of friendship is not words but meanings.

– Henry David Thoreau

Sweet are the uses in adversity when
it shows us the kindness in our
neighbors' hearts.

– LAURA INGALLS WILDER

A friend loves at all times and a brother
is born for adversity.

– PROVERBS 17:17

Thomas Kinkade

There is a friend who sticks closer than a brother.

– Proverbs 18:24

The best mirror is an old friend.

– George Herbert

Behold, if God so loved us, we also ought to love one another.

– 1 John 4:11

# I *have* counted on you like family. Thanks for being there for me during the difficult times.

᷍

_____

_____

_____

_____

_____

_____

_____

_____

_____

_____

_____

I awoke this morning with devout
thanksgiving for my friends, the old
and new.

– Ralph Waldo Emerson

A false friend and a shadow attend only
while the sun shines.

– Benjamin Franklin

A friend you have to buy; enemies you get for nothing.

— JEWISH PROVERB

I read a little verse a few years ago entitled, "If Only We Understood," and the refrain was "We would love each other better, If only we understood." I have forgotten the author… but the refrain comes to my mind every now and then when I hear unkind remarks.

— LAURA INGALLS WILDER.